Welcome To My Bipolar Mind

#PauseReflectMoveForward

Poems of encouragement created specifically for people dealing with anxiety or depression as well as bipolar disorder

Holly DressON NOT Holly DressOFF

Copyright © 2019 Pause Reflect Move Forward, LLC

All rights reserved.

ISBN: 0692175156
ISBN-13: 978-0692175156

DEDICATION
I dedicate this book to the overthinkers of the world

CONTENTS

	Acknowledgments	i
1	Home 8/21/18	Pg #16
2	Forgive 8/22/18	Pg #19
3	Weather 8/23/18	Pg #21
4	Start Over 8/24/18	Pg #23
5	You Deserve It 8/25/18	Pg #27
6	Forward 8/26/18	Pg #31
7	Damage 8/27/18	Pg #34
8	Clap 8/28/18	Pg #37
9	Nothing 8/29/18	Pg #40
10	Training 8/30/18	Pg #44
11	Circle of Life 8/31/18	Pg #47
12	Power 9/1/18	Pg #50

Holly DressON NOT Holly DressOFF

13 Words 9/2/18   Pg #54

14 Rain 9/3/18   Pg #57

15 Peace 9/4/18   Pg #60

16 Up 9/5/18   Pg #64

17 Focus 9/6/18   Pg #67

18 Groups 9/7/18   Pg #71

19 Somebody 9/8/18   Pg #73

20 Shine 9/9/18   Pg #78

21 All That We've Got 9/10/18 Pg #82

22 Passion 9/11/18   Pg #85

23 Insane 9/12/18   Pg #88

24 School 9/13/18   Pg #90

25 The Lost Poem 4/22/19 Pg # 94

26	Plan 9/15/18	Pg #96
27	The Meaning of Life 9/16/18	Pg #99
28	Money 9/17/18	Pg #102
29	Got 9/18/18	Pg #105
30	Impossibe 9/19/18	Pg #109

PREFACE

I'm a writer and I don't type
I mean what's all the hype?
Everyone has always told me what to do and why?
But I don't know unless I try
My talent is typing on my phone with my thumbs
Somehow when I do this, it helps numb
The pain
This is how I've kept sane
I have challenges following directions
Not because I can't read
My brain just doesn't work that way
For as long as I can remember I have always been different
What's the difference?
Not one of us has the same fingerprint
We are all different
People have tried to put me in a box
But I have always thought out of the box
I've been known to be sly as a fox
And paint rocks
One of the problems is, is my throat chakra gets clogged
And I can't breathe
It's like a knot in my throat

I didn't know there were people in the same boat
I've spent my entire life not knowing who I was
I forgot to look in the mirror
To see myself clearer
Now that I have?
I'm going to be unstoppable
Bipolar has had me walk in circles for 42 years
I want to spend the rest of my life fighting it
Learning it
Inside and out
Because no one should be without
Knowledge of knowing oneself
One of my favorite movies is Elf
You see
Bipolar is a roller coaster of emotions
I understand now why I am drawn to oceans
And take showers to try to wash away the pain
Water has drawn me nearer
I find peace
It helps me release
The waves
I crave
I'm doing my best to not misbehave
I need you to understand that this is not just a day to day occurrence
It is a minute by minute endurance

Second by second
Awareness
That I must have
And it's hard to get out
Because when I am there all I feel is doubt
I cannot live without
The help of my family
Yes they've been torn apart
The way I was
Now?
I'm putting my family together like a puzzle
So I won't have to wear a muzzle
This mouth of mine?
Doesn't match my mind
I have to remind myself to be kind
Not just to everyone else
But more importantly
Myself
Or
I'll never be able to place that Emmy on my shelf
I've worked tirelessly to get to where I am at
I cannot digress
I've paused long enough
Reflected entirely too long
I have to keep moving forward

#PAUSEREFLECTMOVEFORWARD

My 1st round of 30 different microphones in 30 days (as of right now there are 2) I started April 18, 2018, which was my 1st book I titled **30 Different Microphones In 30 Days**. The 2nd 30 day challenge I gave myself I decided to name my 2nd book **Welcome To My Bipolar Mind**. I attended all of the open mic nights on my journey by myself except the last ones of each personal challenge. I wanted to prove to myself that I could still write poetry without the help of marijuana. When I wrote each poem in my 1st book, I was under the influence of marijuana.

During both of my challenges I learned to love me. I also learned I enjoy going places by myself without feeling the need for someone else to be there. There are so many people to meet and learn from. It helped me out of my comfort zone to grow and have new experiences, not to mention I had so much fun. Learning to love myself and honor myself has been the best relationship I've ever had.

This book of poems is different from the last. You'll notice my personal growth and understand this journey only if you read my 1st book.

This book just like my 1st book is designed to be read in chronological order. You will notice the 25th poem in this book is out of order. That was my intention. I misplaced the 25th poem during editing for publication, so I created a new one for that day 7 months after the journey was finished. I spent that time over thinking about misplacing it. I decided to move forward and create a new one with the help of an amazing friend.

Just like in the 1st book I wrote each poem the morning of and read it aloud on open mics all over South Florida. I haven't taken prescription medicine in over a year and a half. Alcohol I can't even remember how long that's been. I quit drinking caffeine and smoking marijuana on 7/22/18. I was and still am determined to get me right. I didn't start using marijuana until I was almost 41 and have never tried any other illegal drug. I was 42 during both 30 day challenges I gave myself. I believe I learned my lesson rather quickly.

January of 2017 I was diagnosed with bipolar disorder after an attempted suicide. At that time I couldn't understand why my husband didn't love me the way I felt I needed to be loved. Later realizing he couldn't love me the way I needed to be loved because I hadn't figured out how to love myself.

I didn't understand why I was diagnosed this way and felt the need to explore how and why I did things in my life as well as learning why I didn't do some things that other people would have. Which is why I challenged myself to 2 different 30 day challenges.

Fast forward to August of 2018. I was given a challenge by my childhood friend after I had started my sobriety journey, to do another round of 30 different microphones in 30 days. I remember saying to her "do you know how hard that was and how much work I put into that?" I remember her reminding me that hard work pays off. On the night of my 30th day of sobriety from marijuana I started my 2nd round of 30 different microphones in 30 days which was 8/21/18.

I gave both of these personal challenges to myself to do just that, challenge myself. I wanted to be better and whatever that looked like.

Acknowledgments

My mommy for giving me her strength, who is gone but never forgotten.
My daddy for teaching me how to laugh and move forward, who is gone but never forgotten.
Both of my husbands for our 4 amazing children.
My children for teaching me the gifts of love, hope and faith.
My brother for being my biggest fan now that I can no longer hear the sound of our daddy's voice.

DAY 1
HOME 8/21/18

Taking care of yourself is a full time job
I decided I needed to be sober on top of it
Like I really needed to add that to my plate?
It's never too late
Pot was my drug of choice
And get this
I'm 42 and I didn't start smoking it till I was almost 41!
I'm grateful
Who wouldn't be?
I'll tell you who
Me!
I woke up one morning
31 days ago today
At like 4:30am
Decided to go smoke

Insomnia?
Is no joke
I probably hit it a couple more times than I should have looking back
And when I laid back
In my bed
My heart started pounding through my chest
I thought I was having a heart attack
I text my family 143
I didn't think that this could happen to me
I was so young
Had my oldest daughter of 4 call the ambulance
They took me to the hospital
And before I signed the papers
After they had told me I wasn't having a heart attack ?
I decided to leave
Because I had realized
It was the pot that did it to me
I have bipolar
So I change my mind from time to time
Not to mention how often I rhyme
So what's a gal to do?
To try to make it through?
She adds one more thing to her plate
I don't take prescriptions, smoke, or do drugs, drink alcohol, or drink caffeine
Sometimes I can end up being pretty mean

I pause
Then I reflect
And do my very best to move forward
Towards my dreams
Sometimes it seems
They are out of reach
But by doing these things I listed above
I've taught myself
So now I have to teach
This microphone to me?
Is home

#PAUSEREFLECTMOVEFORWARD

DAY 2
FORGIVE 8/22/18

I can sleep for 5 minutes and it feels like hours
It is one of my super powers
I'm here tonight to remind you to never cower
I know how bad you've been hurt
But hurt?
Is here to make you stronger
Maybe you can't see that right now
So I'm going to remind you how
God already knows your struggle
He has seen you stumble
What He wants to hear is your gratitude
Remember to pause and check your attitude
Before you start pointing fingers
Otherwise the situation lingers

As you reflect
Don't neglect
What you have some people wish they had
I know things have been bad
But once you turn it into glad
Your able to move forward not being mad or sad
We have one life to live
Remember to give
It your best
Your faith?
Will help create
The life you've always wanted
I know how you've been taunted
And deceived
When is the last time you've allowed yourself to receive?
Sometimes we block our blessings
By being hateful
Start being grateful
You won't be misled
Before you close your eyes tonight when you go to bed
Look back at what you did today
If you didn't do anything good for yourself or anyone else
And no one was nice to you
Forgive
#PAUSEREFLECTMOVEFORWARD

DAY 3
WEATHER 8/23/18

L- o-v-e is a four letter word spelled so simply
And felt by me so deeply
I give the love I have inside so freely
I'm doing my best to understand myself completely
Admittedly
I've had people fall in love with me
When I knew we weren't meant to be
In the past I've told people to not fall in love with me
Because I knew at one point or another I would break them completely
It's not because I like to play games
It's because I'm doing my best to stay sane

I've let people go because I know that's the
way that they should go
Still I long for
Appreciation
Acceptance
Acknowledgment
I never meant
To hurt you
But it did happen
I love to hear when people are clapping
The love that I have is like a drug
Once you have me I'm hard to let go
This is why I am on this show
I've learned to let go
So much so
Even though
I wasn't sure which direction to go
So I give myself these challenges
To challenge me
Because I know that I can be better
Through any type of weather

#PAUSEREFLECTMOVEFORWARD
.

DAY 4
START OVER 8/24/18

Ladies
Don't wait for a man to please you
Tease you
Mislead you or
Mistreat you
Love you
I spent a better part of half my life trying to get this right
I fought with all my might
What I should have been doing was flying a kite
Getting to know me
Instead of waiting for him to love me
I'd forgotten
To love me

I didn't honor myself
Take care of myself
Once I started
I was no longer broken hearted?
At 42
I stand before you
To remind you
To take care of you
If it means eating chocolate
Or leaving your man
So you can figure out your plan
I suggest you do it
If he loves you he'll take you back
Please try to relax
I love to listen to a sax
As a matter of fact
I like to listen to instrumental
It's stimulates my mind
And helps me with my rhyme
So I have reason
To figure out this season
Of my life
So I can finally get me right
I hope this stimulates your ear
I believe this is something you need to hear
So when you go home
Even if your all alone
And you go to pick up the phone
To call someone so you won't feel that way

And you realize it's too late to call
Be sure you don't fall
Victim
Of a lonely condition
I give you permission
To please yourself
Not anyone else
What they don't know won't hurt them
What you need to know it's ok to grow
Explore
Give yourself more
Try to adore
Y-o-u
Three letters that mean so much
That actually long for your touch
Whether it's your body
Or your mind
Do what you have to do to have a good time
I talk in rhyme
Because right now?
Is my time to shine
Be sure to pause for even just a moment
To reflect on where you are
I believe you can go far
Move forward towards your dreams
I know how sometimes it seems
Pointless
I promise you it's not
We all tend to get caught

In who we thought we should be right now?
Figure out how
To make some great memories
And cherish the good times
Not the bad
This will help you be glad
Write them down on paper
Even on a wall
We have to see the future
Before we can create it
So when you wake up you'll see it
Over and over
Until one day
You realize
It's ok start over

#PAUSEREFLECTMOVEFORWARD

DAY 5
YOU DESERVE IT 8/25/18

My story is unique to say the least
Diagnosed with bipolar late in life.
Not until 41 did I have an answer
Why my mind thinks faster
The doctor gave me a pill to try to help
But what happened was,
I lost my smile
I would travel mile after mile looking for answers
Looking back?
I'm grateful for him
Not for what he gave me though
A pill?
Compounded in a lab
With toxin and chemical
And him not knowing my chemistry

Only based upon others
All I wanted to do was hide under the covers
So I stopped taking that pill
And another pill I took from the side effects of the first pill
And then another
And then another
It's been over a year now since I stopped taking them
Not to mention I'm currently sober
I don't think anyone can deny what I'm saying
We as a society have to keep paying
If it's not one side effect it's another
And you're telling me we haven't come up with a cure?
The medicine needs refill after refill
They are only giving us a band aid and not helping to cure
From the wealthy to the poor
How much longer do we have to endure?
If you ask me?
More people need to stand up
Just because you can't see your voice doesn't mean it isn't there
You would think that they would care?
Don't you dare
Tell me I'm wrong
Because if you do?
That's ok

I'll still find my way
I don't need you to agree with me
At least listen to me?
What you seek
Is also seeking you
You and I aren't the only ones that are going through
Try tapping
Meditating
Sound healing
Yoga
Eating organic foods
Drinking alkaline water
Saying no to plastic
And get enthusiastic!
About your life
About your family
About all of those that are out there hurting
We need to be helping
If I can do this?
I know you can too
I'll be right here to help you through
I know i only have my voice
But
I'm here to remind you,
You do have a choice
The next time you're at the doctor
Because I'm not telling you shouldn't go
Or to stop all your medicines

That is just something I did
Ask for an alternative
Will it take longer?
Most likely
However
In the long run
It will be worth it
Do you know why?
You deserve it

#PAUSEREFLECTMOVEFORWARD

Day 6
FORWARD 8/26/18

When people hurt?
I hurt
When people smile?
I smile
When people cry?
I cry
When people die?
So does a part of me
I choose to surround myself with life
Flowers and trees
They somehow bring me to my knees
All of people's feelings
Feel
Real to me
I think you would agree
When you see someone laughing
It's contagious

Why not put them on stages?
To help others
Laugh at their problems
Instead of cry
If I cry?
Please help me dry my eye
With a joke
Help me laugh
Because when I get sad
Somehow I end up turning it into mad
Not always
Often enough
I know I am tough
And as I age I've learned I am enough
So I stand up
On this microphone
To tell you
You aren't alone
This big wide world can be intimidating
So I do my best to be less stressed
Naturally
Without all the catastrophe
From prescribed pills
Pills?
Have many people redoing their wills
They weren't expected to die so young
That's the thing about expectations
The doctor says take this
And we hope that it helps

I believe so does he
However
I don't think most docs are thinking clearly
Medicine has been around since the beginning of time
However
Now?
It's easier to take a pill
When your ill
I've never been known to take the easy way out
I've learned to go through my adversities
To receive clarity
On why I did this
And why I did that
And why I saved his cat
I paused just long enough
To be able to reflect
And due to that time
Not only has that time help me rhyme
But more importantly
I've been able to move forward

#PAUSEREFLECTMOVEFORWARD

DAY 7
DAMAGE 8/27/18

Sadness?
Equals madness
I simply don't have the time
So I rhyme
With reason
It is the season
I've forgiven
And I'm still living
I looked for a direction to go
I chose forward
Because bringing up my bad past
Makes my sadness last
I fight with my brain more often than I'd like to admit
Still I don't quit
I'm proving to myself I'm too legit to quit
Moving forward?

Isn't easy
This I know all too well
The gates of hell try to keep me
My demons fight me everyday
Usually at night
I'll find something isn't right
I'm retraining my brain
To keep me from going insane
I've never liked staying in my own lane
When I've stayed where they told me
I go insane
If I move forward they do their best to pull me back
It isn't due to any lack
I tend to get distracted
I still think I'm attractive
Thank goodness I don't look like what I've been through
Sometimes putting on a smile is hard
When I do?
I show the devil that I'm in charge!
He wants to barge
Right in
While he wears that grin
Drooling at the mouth
With a cloud hanging over him with doubt
He invites me
Sometimes I'll admit
It looks like fun

That's when I go run
Or climb stairs
Sometimes it looks like me eating Carmelo's
And taking off all my clothes
The clothes tend to bind me
Then I have to remind me
This isn't who God wants me to be
He wants me to be with my family
Asking them to help
Not anyone else
Not a pill
Or a drink
Even a toke
I use sign language
To manage
It helps prevent any more damage

#PAUSEREFLECTMOVEFORWARD

DAY 8
CLAP 8/28/18

A bit of poetic justice
Ones expectations will lead to disappointment
Pre meditated resentments
Expecting something to happen and it doesn't
You end up taking out on the ones you love
All in God's timing as I've learned
We can't control the future
Most of us can't even control ourselves
So why do we do it?
False hope
How do you cope?
When you thought something was going to happen?
I doubt anyone will be clapping
You end up being upset

Then you let it get to you
No one really knows what you are going through
People have perceptions
Even you don't recognize your own reflection
The doctor will prescribe you medication
And if you chose not to go
It looks like cries
I hope you realize
What you think it will be
Won't
Life is sometimes a joke
Are you working towards that goal?
Or waiting for it to happen?
Me?
I keep tapping
When the reaction happens
Of what you thought isn't
You end up neglecting
The people that are there for you
No matter what your going through
Then they get tired
Please be careful your relationships with them don't end up expired
Because
Repeating the same sad story?
No one will want to be a part of your glory
The friends you expected to be there
Will leave you because they care

About themselves
And they should
It isn't their fault you ended up living in the hood
So appreciate what you have
Work towards what you want
Don't expect it to fall into your lap
If you do?
You won't hear anyone clap

#PAUSEREFLECTMOVEFORWARD

DAY 9
NOTHING 8/29/18

Our communities offer a platform
To creatives
The misfits
The hungry
People who desire change
Those people have courage
Strength unmeasured
And thoughts
Never ending
Why isn't there more?
More people who desire change?
Is it because
They don't want to rearrange?
They'd rather stand and judge?
Will they ever budge?
I smudge
My home

My car
My family
Myself
To get rid of the negative energy
And promote synergy
I can stand up here and speak of madness and sadness
Lord knows I've done it before
Now?
I'd rather speak of hope
To help others cope
I know what it's like to be at the bottom
And claw my way to the top
Moving forward?
I will never stop
Change must happen
Society keeps trying to keep us down
With commercials and social media
Taking advantage of our minds
They are part of the reason I rhyme
I choose to block them out
I do believe there is a way out
When everyone zigs
I like to zag
Even if it's wrong
This helps me feel like I belong
I never planned on this being a song
But if I had the opportunity
I'd sing about unity

About letting go of the past
So we as people can finally be free at last
I never ever thought of myself as political
But if that's what you call it?
I will honor it
My thoughts matter
My truths I believe in
I have a demon
I fight everyday
I know you do too
Mine just so happened to be named bipolar
Yours may be your past?
Or drugs?
Or sadness?
Which can turn into madness
Fight it
Every minute
Every second of everyday
And use your voice for good
Speak of hope
It helps not only yourself
But others be glad
Fight the stigma
I don't wish to be an enigma
But a voice of hope
To fight the pills with the side effects that give us chills
Remind people to control themselves
Not others

Because when you try to control everything
You end up controlling nothing

#PAUSEREFLECTMOVEFORWARD

DAY 10
TRAINING 8/30/18

I'm training myself to be better
It all starts with our brains
As I've come to learn
It leads everything
From when we walk
To what we eat
More importantly the way we think
So I'm starting with my brain
Over the years
I've done my best to fight back the tears
As well as my fears
Sometimes my brain wins
Or does it?
The bipolar part tries to win
I have a war inside my head

Welcome To My Bipolar Mind

Everyday
Every minute
Every second
I do my best to visualize swords
Me against bipolar
My war is within
Maybe you can relate?
When you stay up late
Thinking of what you have to do the next day
Of what you didn't accomplish today
Start feeling sorry for yourself
Because of the cards that you have been dealt
Life is a game
To see who can and won't become insane
Due to living mundane
I tend to use my phone for all my notes that happen in my brain
I seem to deal with short term memory loss
So if I'm driving instead of writing I talk out loud
Even my poems
So I can go back and edit
This morning I left my phone on record while I was driving
I know I'm not the only one
I've caught myself in the act
Bipolar
Not me
You see

I'm aware
My reaction to any given situation is due to what is happening within
Let it out
Even if you have to shout
What's wrong with us inside
Shows on the outside
I'm doing my best to abide
I think we all should
However, I never liked that word should
We could
But will we?
That's up to me
And you
Whatever it is we are going through
Control yourself
Nothing else
Re-training

#PAUSEREFLECTMOVEFORWARD

DAY 11
CIRCLE OF LIFE 8/31/18

Will certainly do it's best to knock you down
I know how hard it is to get back up
We meet the people that come into our life
for a reason, a season, or lifetime
God leaves it up to us to decide which
He thinks we're so smart
Sometimes I wonder if he's just up there
shaking his head at me
I'm doing my best to just let things be
It's interesting how life happens
And interesting who happens to stay
As well as who happens to go
There have been times when I've wanted to
throw
Everything away

Including myself
The devil will do it's best to keep you down
Make you wear a frown
You must always remember to straighten your crown
The devil does not want you to succeed
At anything you do
No matter what it is you're going through
Keep your eyes
On your prize
And whatever that looks like to you
Not anyone else
There will be cheerleaders
Naysayers
The nonbelievers
As well as the relievers
So what do you do to move forward?
You stand and fight
With all of your might
Believe in yourself
Let go of the doubt
Cleanse your home
Of clutter
Of things that don't mean anything to you
I believe things hold energy
Good and bad
It's up to you decide which things will make you glad
I know you've had

Things in the past that have made you sad
As well as mad
Do what you have to do to make yourself glad
For me it's writing and cleaning
Oddly enough
When I clean up
And get rid of stuff
I have better luck
I know how sometimes you get stuck
And that's ok
Because at the end of the day
You've done what you could
With what you knew
Find positive affirmations
And stick to them like glue
Don't you think it is long overdue?
The things you do for others
Will end up coming back to you
This is the circle of life

#PAUSEREFLECTMOVEFORWARD

DAY 12
POWER 9/1/18

Somewhere along my way I lost mine
No
Not my electricity
My inner power
My mind seemed to never figure that out
Growing up I had so much doubt
I'm still growing
And have experienced this as an adult
There is always something new to learn
Not one person knows everything
Accept the big man himself
How does one grow?
For me?
I asked myself questions
And instead of asking others

I'd ask the internet
Go to the library and read
And then
Came to my own conclusions
Society is filled with so many delusions
And then we somehow have to make sense of them
I remember when I was in college and the math professor asked me to stop asking questions
Told me "I was confusing people"
If you ask me
He was the one with uncertainty
I was there to learn
He may have been there for a paycheck
I didn't go back after that
Told myself he was right
When now as I've learned he wasn't
Why we hear others negative opinions and not hear the positive and listen to those?
Only each of us knows
Ourselves
Or do we?
How many people actually know themselves completely?
If you ask me
My answer is
Not enough
God built us to be tough

We all have challenges in our lives
He wants us to get it right
To teach ourselves
And then teach others
Not hide under the covers
There is this big wide world out there to explore
I suggest you adore
You
After all you've been through
Don't you think you owe it to yourself?
To try
To love you
Your worthy
Of all you've ever dreamed of
But if you don't love and honor yourself
How do you expect anyone else to?
Sometime the world hands us poo
All I'm suggesting
Is that you continue
To discover you
Why you do this
Why you do that
Why you don't do this
Why you don't do that
As a matter of fact
Now that I'm
Mentioning it
I bet your considering it

Welcome To My Bipolar Mind

Your reading or listening to this poem for a reason
At this exact moment
This is the sign you've been looking for
I know when you walked through that door
You couldn't have possible imagined hearing these words
You can earn those rewards
When you walk up to the pearly gates
You'll realize you are there because of fate
Don't wait until it's too late
Appreciate
You
Him or her
You can conquer
The ups
The downs
The in-betweens
Be open to the open mic scene
There is so much talent out there
And in you
Continue
To find you
And whatever that looks like to you
Don't relinquish your power

#PAUSEREFLECTMOVEFORWARD

DAY 13
WORDS 9/2/18

I have words in my head
As soon as I get out of bed
As well as when I lay my head
Including during the day
Whether it's morning
Or mid-day
Or even evening
I've learned to keep believing
To do what I can to make sense of all the words
And fight bipolar with make believe swords
The rewards?
Endurance
Perseverance
To fight loneliness
Social media is a lie

All the likes
Something isn't right
We need more connection
As well as affection
I have two maybe three people that i believe i can talk to
Not many check on me
Because I'm the strong one
Due to what happened in the past
My mouth speaks too fast
So I'm doing my best to pause
I had to figure out how to receive applause
You see
Not many people understand me
Nor do I really need them to
It would be nice if someone dropped me a hello
I'd like to think I was a friendly fellow
I'm mellow at times
Then I'm high
I feel as if I can fly
No drug is needed
I have succeeded
At managing myself
And have learned my health especially my mental health?
Is my wealth
I'm deserving of all my dreams
Sometimes it seems

They aren't attainable
And I am unmanageable
I somehow figure it out
Sometimes it happens when I clean grout
I cannot live without
Growing
It keeps me yearning
And my wheels turning
I have this burning
Inside of me
I know I'm not the only one
My time?
Isn't done

#PAUSEREFLECTMOVEFORWARD

DAY 14
RAIN 9/3/18

Listening and watching the rain
For me somehow lessons the pain
It brings me hope
Knowing it won't last
And helps the flowers grow
My life has seen some rain
Thank goodness it doesn't last
The situations ends
The story remains
Somehow I'm left to refrain
From thinking about it
Over and over
Even though it's gone
Something inside me helps it linger
I never really did like ginger
I used to point my finger
At what he'd done
What she didn't do

And then realized there were 3 more fingers pointing back at me
You see
I didn't realize myself
That I was part of the problem
I didn't know
Even though
I look in the mirror quite often
I didn't ask myself the important questions
And waited to hear their mentions
My intentions?
Were never to hurt anyone
Yet somehow I did
And now I'm trying to make things right
Which is why I write
It helps me see my thoughts clearer
So my days become less drearier
I felt inferior
To everyone
I guess you could say I faked it till I could make it
Not in business
But in life
I'm doing my best to get me right
So I stand and fight
With what's going on inside of me
And remind me
To love me completely
I write frequently

Welcome To My Bipolar Mind

Sometimes it doesn't make sense
By doing this I've become a professional thumb typer
Sometimes I get hyper
Then I get sad
And have managed to turn it into glad
My life isn't so bad
I know you aren't supposed to compare your life to others
I still miss my brothers
I'm doing my best to recover
And I know my best can be better
Through any kind of weather
When the rain stops
There is a rainbow
The flowers grow
I think there's something you need to know
What you've been through is ok
What you're going through?
You'll make it
Where you are going?
Keep your eyes on your prize
You will realize
Your dreams can come true
You will make it through
The rain?
Will grow a better you

#PAUSEREFLECTMOVEFORWARD

DAY 15
PEACE 9/4/18

I looked for it everywhere
I listened to what everybody said but I didn't hear them.
It's not like I didn't care
I simply wasn't ready to be aware
It has taken so much time
What helped me was me working on my rhyme
I learned to look in the mirror
To see myself clearer
The reflection that I was looking at I didn't recognize
I had to close my eyes
I had to stop all the endless chatter that happened in my mind
And learned that my thoughts matter

But what I've learned is that I don't have to think what I'm thinking I can change it like a mad hatter
Once I became aware
I began to dare
To do the impossible
And make it possible
I had to push myself each day
Because some days
Bipolar would tell me not to and leave me in a haze
Bipolar has tried to keep me down for days
I've had to fight him or her to do the things that I believe are important
Not what it wants me to do
I had to learn about myself through and through
Thank goodness for my daughter Drew
And my daughters Destiny and Jazmyn and my son DJ
My daddy
And my brother
They love me like no other
They stood beside me and behind me when others didn't
I was too much for some
When I came undone
I'd tell my story of sadness
Here there

And everywhere
To anyone that would listen
I verbal vomited on everyone
Sometimes I can't believe what I have done
I've learned that God has forgiven me
So I forgave me
The people that have not forgiven me?
That says something more about them
Than it does about me
We all love differently
Admittedly
Some of the things I have done I wouldn't have done to my worst enemy
Since I've paused
And had some time to reflect
I've learned that my worst enemy is in me
Once I recognized this I was able to move forward
Toward
What I believe is important
Mental health is our wealth
And the sooner we recognize this within ourselves
The better off we will all be
Give it a try
I know you will see
Peace is within you
Ask peace out for a cup of decaf coffee
Maybe add pumpkin spice it certainly is nice

or coconut cream?
That will help you reach your dream
Once we stop giving our bodies the chemicals
and the things that it doesn't need
We as a human race will be able to succeed
My wish for you?
I wish you peace
Within yourself
And realize your mental health
Is your wealth

#PAUSEREFLECTMOVEFORWARD

Day 16
UP 9/5/18

My head has been shaved
My eyes have seen heartache
My ears have heard words they wish they never heard
My sense of smell?
Boy I have some stories I could tell
My mouth has said things that shouldn't have been said
My shoulders have carried the weight of the world
My heart has been broken
My back has carried 4 children
My legs have walked miles
My knees have knelt in the grass
My feet have run marathons
My mind has thought things it should have never thought
Somehow
I fought

We have all had things happen to us which we wish didn't happen
Yet
We continue on
I wake at dawn
And tell the Lord I'm grateful
I do my best not to ever be hateful
I share this with you
Because
Believe it or not
I'm just like you
Our voices?
We need to use them for good
Stop
Being
Ungrateful
What you have?
Others pray to have
That Emmy I'm reaching for is up for grabs
The books that I write
I hope when you read them at night
You smile
Or chuckle
Or maybe
Just maybe
Realize
You aren't alone
As I am
On this microphone

I have this opportunity
To say whatever I want
Whether you like it or not
I'm taking my shot
And I'm giving you
All
That
I've
Got!
When you see your neighbor wave hello
Life is too short to be shallow
When you look in the mirror ask yourself the questions that you're dying to know the answers to
I believe all of the answers are inside of you
You have to put down everything every once in a while
Take yourself on a walk
And if you travel mile after mile?
And You still don't find the answers that you're looking for?
Keep looking
Keep asking questions
Don't
Ever
Give
Up

#PAUSEREFLECTMOVEFORWARD

Day 17
FOCUS 9/6/18

Focus?
Have you lost it?
I'm reminding you that it can't be found.
It is there
However you have to do the work
No not your j-o-b
The work has to be done in you.
You see
I've gotten myself into a situation a time or two with relationships
Whether with my family or my friends or intimate relationships and I've lost focus.
I've pointed out what the other person did
And said things such as "I can't believe they did that to me! Or why would they say that? Or I don't understand why this keeps happening?"
You see what ended up happening

When I came to this awareness
Was that it wasn't them, it was me
I was so busy pointing fingers at all the things that people would do to me and never paid any attention to what I was doing to them
So I had to work
On me
I lost my focus
In me
I was so focused on everyone else
And what everybody else was doing or wasn't doing
And I wasn't taking any time to figure out why I was doing what I was doing or not for that matter
Does anybody really know themselves?
You can't if you don't do the work.
We all carry around these ideas of what we are supposed to have our life look like from what we were taught
From our friends
And we forgot to look at ourselves
And ask ourselves what we wanted
What we want most in life?
What makes us happy?
What makes us sad?
What makes us angry?
What makes us happy?
What makes us love?

And it's so important for us to pay attention
to those things because what happens is
You lose yourself and everyone else
I'm grateful for the mistakes that I've made
because they taught me to learn how to make
the right decisions.
Even though those right decisions are harder
or more challenging
I've done them anyways.
I've written things in the past and look back
over them
And realized how much I've grown as a
human being
We can no longer keep being the way we
always have
Because we will continue to get what we've
always gotten.
If we want something different we have to
make different choices
If we continue to do the same thing over and
over again?
Expecting a different result?
That my friend is called insanity
And if you look at the spelling of that word
INsane
I-N is in the beginning of it
There are signs all around us
And we often don't pay any attention to them
but when we are open and aware

We are able to receive all the things that are heart desires
But
If we keep pointing fingers at the things that have been done to us and people who have done us wrong
We focus more on them than on ourselves
Those terrible things happened for us
Not to us
One day you'll figure out why
Maybe you never will
It's important to pause long enough
To spend some time doing self-reflection
To be able to move forward
And once we start realizing this?
We grow
Not just as people
As a community
It creates unity
I invite you to do as I've done
I had to re-focus

#PAUSEREFLECTMOVEFORWARD

Day 18
GROUPS 9/7/18

Are you in any groups on social media?
Some that are positive?
Maybe some that are negative?
A couple of the groups I am in are based upon bipolar because the doctors tell me that is what I have
Most of the groups I am in believe that bipolar is their weakness
I don't
I believe that bipolar is my strength and my gift from God
Bipolar is a mental illness that has up and down emotions
I can be extremely happy and I can be extremely depressed all within a minutes time
Somedays trying mange?
Is harder than others

I had one of those days yesterday

#PAUSEREFLECTMOVEFORWARD

Day 19
SOMBODY 9/8/18

Please don't
Judge me
You may
Just nudge me
Into making more of my dreams a reality
What's happened in my past?
Is there for good
No longer will I feel like I'm
Not any good
The worthlessness that comes from having bipolar?
Is being thrown over my shoulder
Now that I'm older

And sober?
I'm open to see
That anything I want
Can be
Admittedly
It has taken me so long
To find out that I belong
I know in my heart this feeling
Can't be wrong
I deserve to be here
And so do you
Together?
We can make it through
Turn your blue?
Into blue skies
The fire in your soul?
Into cries
Of gratefulness
And perseverance
It will make your demons shy away
They never could have imagined this day
When they are conquered
You can win
And you will
I will NOT take that pill
It makes me ill
And gives me a chill
I'd much rather have a thrill
Wouldn't you?

Don't continue
To have the same sad story repeated in your head
I know there are days that you dread
And sometimes having to give them what they want fed
Is easier
When it comes to anxiety and
Depression?
I have a confession
It is easier to take a pill
I'd rather fight my demons naturally
Because I'm not going to kill my immune system
What's left of it anyways
When I manage this way
I'm learning to live
With the life that He gave me
Bipolar
I'm standing right here
Give me your best shot
I'm giving my life all that I've got
You can make me look like a fool
I will continue to make you drool
You are ugly
God?
Doesn't like ugly
And neither do I
All you ever want to do is pry

And make me cry
I can't deny
You have succeeded in my past
This time?
I'm telling you it will not last
You can keep trying to cast
Your reel
And do your best to make me feel
Like I'm not good enough
This time around I'll show you just how tough
I am
I know I can
Beat you
And I'll laugh in your face
And make you taste
The bitterness of your soul
This is my goal
I am nice
I've even been told that my kindness is my weakness
This time around at the Preakness?
I will win
You can keep your gin
And your pills
And your caffeine
And that bad weed that I smoked
You have provoked
In me
A commotion

Even though in the past I've been scared of the ocean
Watch me make waves
You tell the rest of them to run back to their cage
Because I'm throwing away the key for good
You have made me cry my last tear
I don't have any fear
My name is pronounced
Holly DressON NOT Holly DressOFF
In case you don't know how to spell it
You better ask somebody

#PAUSEREFLECTMOVEFORWARD

Day 20
SHINE 9/9/18

If you tell yourself you can't
Guess what?
You won't
But if you tell yourself you can?
You will!
Which declaration will you make for yourself today?
If you don't
How much longer are you willing to pay?
The price
Of simply getting by
By being nice?
And see where it gets you?

You don't have to continue
Going through
Life as you have always known it
It is time
To own it
What's happened in your past?
Happened for a reason
This is your season
To do
Whatever you want
You are not supposed to live your life in want
What you want?
Is out there waiting for you
Don't continue
To do as you have always done
Because the dreams you only dream of?
You'll end up with none
I know sometimes you think you should have won
I say?
Fail to reach success!
Without it
You'll never get what you feel you deserve by not getting whatever is holding you back off your chest
Less is more
More is there
Why don't you at least try to pretend that you care?

The love affair
With him or her?
Why not fall in love with you?
We cannot continue
To do what we have always done
And expect more
We've got to do things that we haven't done
Once you do
You'll see
And believe me
You will
Give yourself a try
We were not made to just get by
But to thrive
And live
And give with an open heart
Haven't you learned your part?
If not
I suggest you learn
Then you will feel the burn
The sensation
And resist temptation
When you fall in love with yourself
You will no longer need medication
Whether it is a pill
Or alcohol
Or even drugs
Give yourself a hug
And start to receive

All
That you were made to be
Admittedly
It has taken me quite sometime
To figure me out
But once I did
I let go of all my doubt
This?
Is my time to shine

#PAUSEREFLECTMOVEFORWARD

Day 21
ALL That We've Got 9/10/18

I think suicide is one of those words
One hopes to never hear
We can't keep living our lives in fear
Today I've had my ups and my downs
Looking at the reality of suicide
And mental illnesses
That so many of us face
Whether it is me looking at my face
Or hearing through a text
That someone is gone
Due to an overdose
I feel the tingling in my toes
It flows through my veins up to my nose

And then the story goes
To my mind
Through my mind
And then I remember
When I thought about doing it too
Social media makes it look like we have so many friends
But
As I'm sure you've learned
It never ends
I sometimes pretend
That I hear a ding
Or a ring
And
You know what?
Sometimes it never comes
And that's okay
Because at the end of the day
I like me!
Really?
I love me!
Maybe for not some of the things that I've done
But I have forgiven me
Maybe you need to too
The reality is
That nobody knows what you are going through
And honestly they don't need to know

It's time for you to grow
And blossom
And stop playing possum!
It is time we all live our lives
Because
Why not?
Let's give it all that we've got!

#PAUSEREFLECTMOVEFORWARD

Day 22
PASSION 9/11/18

Do it with passion
Or not at all
After all
Isn't that how we were made?
We should be lighting our lives up like
Thomas Kinkaid
Yet most of us are only thinking about the
next time we are getting paid
Every once in a while it is ok to misbehave
I'm not suggesting a parade
Hang on a second while I check my fade
If something isn't making you jump out of
bed in the morning
Have you asked yourself what are you doing?

We have one shot
Maybe you forgot
I'm reminding you
To set some goals
And have them stick to you like glue
Don't wait for the residue
To set in
Just begin
It is never too late
Don't live your life like you are in a crate
Create
What you wish for
And make it happen
Don't spend your life napping
Every once in a while yes
But looking forward to napping?
Isn't exactly how life will happen
Risks
And dreams
Hopes
And wishes
I know the least of your favorite this is doing dishes
We all have things we have to get done
Why haven't your wishes begun?
You can read self-help books
Attend seminars
Drive from coast to coast in our cars
But if we don't apply what we learned

What was the point of learning it anyway?
Don't you pray for the day
That all your hopes and dreams come true?
Please don't continue
To point fingers
At him or her
How much longer will you endure?
Life passing you by?

#PAUSEREFLECTMOVEFORWARD

Day 23
INSANE 9/12/18

If you could tell your younger self one thing what would you say?
I answered this myself today
Welcome to my bipolar mind
I'd tell myself
"Your brain will try to trick you"
Be careful what you say to it
What you think you will manifest
It is almost like a test
God wants to see with your free will if you choose wisely
If decide to follow your heart
Your brain will try to make you go insane
If you allow it

Listen to what I'm saying (as I'm shaking myself)
Don't allow it!
Learn how your brain works
What makes it happy
Angry
Sad
Mad
Lonely
Discouraged
Encouraged
Loved
It is the most complex organ in your entire body
Don't ever try to be like anybody
Learn who you are and what you stand for
Believe in yourself
You will go so far
Don't wait for other to approve your thoughts
You'll end up getting caught
In a web of lies
And no one will be there to hear your cries
Monetize
Your assets
Which is your brain
This way you will have no one to blame
And will help you from going insane

#PAUSEREFLECTMOVEFORWARD

Day 24
SCHOOL 9/13/18

One of the things I have always been good at
Is making boys drool
As well as men
I've always seemed to grab their attention
But you see
What was actually happening?
I needed to learn
I wasn't ever taught self-love
Not that I remember anyways
I used to walk into a room and wonder if people like me
Now?
I wonder if I like them

I no longer need their attention
I've learned to be happy
With me
With who I am
And prove to myself
That I can
Have
Whatever it is that I want in life
Once I became a wife
The 1st time at 19
I thought that the role
That I was supposed to play
Was listening to what others had to say
I didn't listen to myself
One of my favorite movies is Elf
You see
I love to smile
But
I lost it along my way
I'm happy to say
I found it
While finding me
No longer do I wait to see
If they like me
Because I like me
In fact
I love me
Completely
I know I can always be better

And get through any storm
I will beat any type of weather
One of my strengths?
Is
Being strong
My list goes on and on
There has been a time when I have been wrong
Ok
Many
But I had to do wrong to know what right is
Pay attention
There is going to be a quiz
There should be classes in school
To teach their kids how to love themselves
Before anyone else
History is important
So is math
As well as English
Why don't we teach them to learn about themselves?
Because as parents
Sometimes
We don't know how to love ourselves
And that's why we all went to school
To learn
Let's light up their souls
And teach them to burn
This way

They can learn
And won't yearn
For others to love them
Teach them
To be their own best friend
Don't you think this is worth teaching a class in school?

#PAUSEREFLECTMOVEFORWARD

Day 25
THE LOST POEM 4/22/19

I held myself back
From reaching one of my goals
Due to a technicality
When in reality
I made a bigger deal about it than I really should have
I have never liked the word should
"I could"
"I can"
"I will"
When you look around life is a thrill
Our thoughts get in the way
Feelings are just feelings they aren't meant to stay
They come and go like seasons
I know we each have our own reasons
For staying where we are
Not going where we have been led

Due to what our brains have been fed
Society will let you down
Turn your frown
Upside down
Your past does not define you
Remind you
The next time you look in the mirror
Say to yourself
"I cannot live my life in fear"

#PAUSEREFLECTMOVEFORWARD

Day 26
PLAN 9/15/18

Thank you Lord for my rest
I have some things I have to get off my chest
I am a sinner
However
I still believe I'm a winner
There are some people in my life
That have chosen not to forgive me
I thank you for never forsaking me
They give me their cold shoulder
While I push this boulder
You see
I have forgiven me
They have yet to
Maybe if you get to?
Help them understand

Welcome To My Bipolar Mind

That what happened
Wasn't part of the plan
Maybe it was?
I believe bad things have to happen
In order to see the good
I'm grateful for You
You've given me some things in my life
That I don't believe many can handle
From the sexual abuse
To the scandal
From the judgments
To the times when all I had was You
Somehow?
Someway?
You helped me push through
To the time
Well, let's be honest
The times when I didn't think I wanted to continue
You rose me up
After I had fallen to my knees
You've had people over seas
Help them see
That I'm not as bad as they say that I am
And remind me
I am an more than enough
You see
Without me
There wouldn't be

4 amazing children
To walk this Earth
There was no one else equipped to handle their birth
I'm grateful
For the people that are hateful
They've taught me
How I never want to be
I've accepted my flaws
Yet
They
Hold onto them
And haven't forgive me
As You have
Help them to understand
That I am only human
Remind them of Your words
And ask them to put down their swords
Because the brain that you gave me
Has tried to enslave me
But I've learned
You forgave me
So I forgave me
I never intended to behave badly
Can you help them understand?
So I can finish Your plan?

#PAUSEREFLECTMOVEFORWARD

Day 27
THE MEANING OF LIFE 9/16/18

As it turns out
We give life meaning
The thoughts in our head
When we are in bed
Or during the day
Say
Live
Which is why we are all different
I like this
You like that
In fact
No two people are alike
Some may want to ride a half pike
Another strum a guitar with a broken finger
Or write words
To fight oncoming swords
No matter what you choose

You never lose
Because you see
Time goes on
No matter what you choose
Make sure you choose something
To make a difference in this world while you are here
Hold onto your passion
Without fear
Because fear?
Is a liar
I'm sure you can hire
Anyone to teach you what you want to learn
Or teach yourself
But
You'll go further with help
We weren't born alone
Our mother was there
Maybe our father
Some don't bother
Thinking of how it all started
And walk around broken hearted
Love was given
And may have not been returned
I know you've yearned
Feel that burn
The fire in your soul
Sometimes takes a toll
You were given this role

You get to choose
Which role you want to play
But whatever it is you choose
At the end of the day
Make sure you are happy
That
Is the meaning of life
Because anything other than that?
Is crap

#PAUSEREFLECTMOVEFORWARD

Day 28
MONEY 9/17/18

You hear people say "I can't wait to get my paycheck"
Or "my money"
When in reality
Money isn't ours
The people that are attached to money?
Are missing out on other opportunities
Such as unity
When two forces
Become one
You find that relationships
Are second to none
That money
Cannot buy happiness
Yes
Having it makes life a bit easier
But has having it actually made you happy?

Are you happy with yourself?
When one looks for happiness with having money
It takes away an opportunity to create more in one's life
Money?
Will never get you right
The only thing that can make you happy is you
Don't continue
To wait
It may be too late
To learn
The best thing to earn
Is love
Which money cannot buy
Don't deny
What makes you happy most
You can travel from coast to coast
Even toast
To your success
But if you don't caress
Your feelings
You may wind up feeling
Alone
Stressed
Anxious
And broken
Please take this token

A suggestion if you will
Don't look for happiness in a pill
It may give you a chill
Toast to your past
And tell it to kiss you're a--
You are full of sass
And are not defined by other people's opinions
Being happy is your decision
To cure what you feel you lack
Give
If you need money
Give
Believe me when I tell you this
Money?
Only helps you live
To have it
You must give

#PAUSEREFLECTMOVEFORWARD

Day 29
GOT 9/18/18

If you don't stand up and use your voice for something that you believe in, you might as well put tape over your mouth and say nothing at all
What happens when you do this is you begin to taste
How bitter you're words inside your mind and your mouth are
Maybe you can relate?
That this is what happened to you in the past?
And then your mind thinks fast?
Then faster
Let's concentrate
Otherwise
You'll end up creating a disaster
In your mind
It repeats in your head over and over again

You begin to talk to others about what your problems are
And end up winding up hiding under the covers
Trying to forget who you are
You are a force
Do what you have to do to stay on course
You will never ever be able to force
Anyone to do what you want them to do
They have to be willing
The thought of them not doing what you want?
May be chilling
However, this is your life
You have to fight for what you believe is right
Don't ever listen to other people's opinions of you
If you do?
You will never make it through
You'll look back on your life
And you'll wish you did things differently
That pill that you're taking to manage your anxiety or your depression?
I have a confession
It is continuing to make you sick
It is suppressing your feelings
The feelings that you're feeling
I believe
You need to be kneeling

Asking whoever you believe created the heavens and the earth
Then finding that answer within yourself
You cannot continue to keep dealing
With what he said or she said
He did or didn't do
What she did or didn't do
Life?
Is about you
You may be a mother
A father
A sister
A brother
I beg of you
Love yourself like no other
Discover
You!
And all you wish to do
Create the life you've always wanted
I know there have been others that have flaunted
Their lives in front of you
You cannot continue
To only cheer other people on
You have to cheer for you
And if the people around you aren't cheering for you too?
Either you continue
Or you pick up the crown on the ground that

you dropped
You place it back on your head
So when you go to bed
You can forgive
Yourself
Like no one else
And fight for you
So you can continue
We get one shot
Give it all you've got

#PAUSEREFLECTMOVEFORWARD

Day 30
IMPOSSIBLE 9/19/18

My bucket list changed over the years
I used to want diamonds and gold
Now I realize they were petty
I hope your ready
Because my bucket list has changed
And my mind has been rearranged
I have changed
I believe for the better
And now know I can make it through any kind of weather
I'm not sure about the cold
Because of the stories I've been told
I suppose someday
I will see the day
When snowflakes fall
After the season of fall

I've always appreciated things that are tall
The trees that He made
Help me to understand
That growth is possible
Even in the tiniest of places
He can see our faces
And tell
What story we tell
And the one we are actually living
He believes in giving
But first you must know the meaning of life
And do what you can to get you right
Don't give up your fight
Keep fighting for what you believe in
He has seen you sin
Now?
He wants to see you grin
Because of what you've made possible
Out of the impossible

#PAUSEREFLECTMOVEFORWARD

BONUS poem

MY LAST

My brain doesn't remember things
Unless there is a picture attached
Why would God want to snatch
That away from me
I've asked myself before why has bipolar happened to me?
I've learned
Time after time
That it happened for me
That bipolar is my strength
Not my weakness
I am here to make a difference!
My mental health?
Is my wealth
My whole life I've dealt
With things happening
And me not knowing what was actually happening

Holly DressON NOT Holly DressOFF

They misdiagnosed me
I was left empty
Now?
I've made myself whole
I have this role
Of being a daughter, a sister, a wife 2 times, a mother four tunes and a friend
Yes I know you hear my voice as it climbs
This?
Is my time to shine
I made this rhyme
For you to look around
At your sister, mother or friend
To help lend
Them your hand
Maybe even a hug
While this mental illness tugs
At my heart
I promise every night to God I'll do my best to play my part
That He gave ne
So bipolar?
Wont enslave me
Even though I've been told I share too much
This microphone?
I have to clutch
Maybe it isn't much
Better than a gun exploding
Or a noose

Or a cut
Or just simply giving up
I stand before you
Without prescriptions
Without drugs
Without caffeine
Without alcohol
You?
May have seen me fall
Now?
I stand so flipping tall
Maybe you recall
A poem I've done in my past
I promise you this
This one?
Won't be my last

#PAUSEREFLECTMOVEFORWARD

About the author

Holly DressON NOT Holly DressOFF's mission is to help people move forward from what is holding them back without other people's opinions and judgments getting in the way. She believes Pause Reflect Move Forward can be applied to all aspects of your life. And Feels it is essential to apply #PauseReflectMoveForward to the life you've always dreamed of, follow the #30DifferentMicrophonesIn30Days and on social media.
For her blogs and merchandise visit

www.PauseReflectMoveForward.com

58094068R00069

Made in the USA
Columbia, SC
17 May 2019